BLS WORKING PAPERS

 U.S. DEPARTMENT OF LABOR
Bureau of Labor Statistics

OFFICE OF PRICES AND LIVING
CONDITIONS

Transfer Pricing, Intrafirm Trade and the BLS
International Price Program

Lorraine Eden, Texas A&M University

Working Paper 334
January 2001

The views expressed are those of the author and do not necessarily reflect the policies of the U.S. Bureau of Labor Statistics or the views of other staff members.   This paper was part of the U.S. Bureau of Labor Statistics Conference on *Issues in Measuring Price Change and Consumption* in Washington, DC, June 2000.

July 2000

TRANSFER PRICING, INTRAFIRM TRADE AND THE

THE BLS INTERNATIONAL PRICE PROGRAM

Lorraine Eden
Associate Professor of Management
Texas A&M University
4221 TAMU
College Station, Texas 77843-4221.
Phone 979-862-4053; fax 409-845-9641.
Email: leden@tamu.edu

Abstract

Most governments keep balance of payments statistics on exports and imports, by value, and construct international prices indexes in order to deflate these statistics. How can intrafirm trade, trade between related parties, bias the construction of these international price indexes? Does transfer pricing, the prices of products traded between related party firms, bias the export and import price indexes in any predictable fashion? If firms manipulate transfer prices to avoid taxes or tariffs, what is the appropriate transfer price to use in constructing export and import price indexes, in theory and in practice? These issues are important because related party trade is huge, representing half of US imports and one-third of US exports, and perhaps a third of worldwide merchandise trade flows. This paper explains how transfer pricing and intrafirm trade can bias the construction of export and import price indexes, outlines and evaluates the various prices that could be used to construct these indexes, and makes some recommendations for the international price program run by the US Bureau of Labor Statistics.

Acknowledgements: An earlier version of this paper was presented at the Bureau of Labor Statistics Conference on *Issues in Measuring Price Change and Consumption* in Washington, DC, June 5-8, 2000. I would like to thank the session chair, William Alterman, for suggesting this topic and for regular and helpful advice during the project, and my discussant, William Randolph, for his insightful comments at the session. Helpful discussions with Kenneth Borghese, Kimberly Clausing, Thomas Connor, Erwin Diewert, Subi Rangan and Jeannette Siegel also improved the paper. All remaining errors are my responsibility.

TRANSFER PRICING, INTRAFIRM TRADE AND THE

BLS INTERNATIONAL PRICE PROGRAM

INTRODUCTION

Most governments keep balance of payments statistics on exports and imports, by value, and construct international prices indexes in order to deflate these statistics. How can *intrafirm trade (IFT)*, trade between related parties such as multinational enterprises (MNEs), bias the construction of these international price indexes? Economists have known for many years that the prices set by MNEs for intrafirm transfers -- *transfer prices* --- are normally *not* the prices that would be negotiated between arm's length parties (Diewert 1985, Eden 1985, Horst 1971). Does transfer pricing bias the export and import price indexes in any predictable fashion? If firms manipulate transfer prices to avoid taxes or tariffs, what is the appropriate transfer price to use in constructing export and import price indexes, in theory and in practice? These issues are important because related party trade is huge, representing half of US imports and one-third of US exports, and perhaps a third of worldwide merchandise trade flows.

This paper is designed to be a preliminary exploration of these questions. The paper explains how transfer pricing and intrafirm trade can bias the construction of export and import price indexes, outlines and evaluates the various prices that could be used to construct these indexes, and makes a variety of recommendations for the international price program run by the US Bureau of Labor Statistics.

The paper is divided into six parts. Part I reviews the literature on the importance and characteristics of intrafirm firm trade, focusing on US data. Part II reviews the current Bureau of Labor Statistics (BLS) international price program. Part III uses a simple heuristic example to

1

show the possible alternative price indexes that could be constructed as a product moves from the factory gate in the exporting country to the retail level in the importing country, and then compares these prices to those currently used by the IPP. Part IV develops a theoretical model of international intrafirm trade between two related parties, comparing the multinational enterprise's profit-maximizing volume and pricing outcomes with the outcomes from international trade between arm's length firms, introducing complications such as tax differentials and tariffs. We conclude this section by asking how transfer pricing and intrafirm trade should, in theory, affect the calculation of international price indexes. Part V moves from theory to practice, focusing on the actual transfer pricing policies of US Customs and the Internal Revenue Service. We show how the international norm of the arm's length standard, as proxied by three transfer pricing methods – comparable uncontrolled price, resale price and cost plus – reflects the MNE's efficient transfer pricing policy. We develop a comparison of the two transfer pricing programs, US Customs and the Internal Revenue Service, that enables us to answer the practical question of which source of transfer pricing data is more appropriate for the BLS international price indexes. The paper concludes by summarizing the theoretical and practical implications of intrafirm trade for the BLS international price program.

THE IMPORTANCE OF INTRAFIRM TRADE

Perhaps half of all international trade in goods and services in the world economy is now conducted through multinational enterprises (MNEs). More than half of that trade is conducted within the MNEs themselves as affiliates in one country trade unfinished and finished goods, services and intangibles with their parents and sister affiliates in other countries. Understanding *international intrafirm trade (IFT)*, trade between related party firms, in terms of its size, growth rates and effects on the national and global economy, is an important topic for academic researchers (see, for example, Bonturi & Fukasaku, 1993; Clausing, 2000; Eden, 1998: Ch.4; Encarnation, 1993; Hipple, 1990a,b; Rangan, 2000). Government researchers have also been interested measuring intrafirm trade (Covari & Wisner, 1993; Mataloni, 1997; UNCTAD, 1999; Whichard & Lowe, 1995, 1998; Zeile, 1997), as have private sector groups (Ernst & Young, 1999; Krajewski, 1992).

Some of the conclusions with respect to US intrafirm trade emerging from this literature are the following:

- In 1999, related party trade accounted for 47% of US merchandise imports and 32% of merchandise exports, by value. Related party trade includes both US companies trading with their foreign affiliates and US subsidiaries of foreign companies trading with their foreign parents (US Census, 2000).

- The share of intrafirm trade in total US merchandise trade varies significantly by country. The shares of the top US trading partners are: Canada (43% of imports, 42% of exports), Japan (74% of imports, 36% of imports), Mexico (66% of imports, 44% of exports), European Union (52% of imports, 31% of exports) (US Census, 2000).

- The share of intrafirm trade in US non-coal, non-petroleum manufacturing exports rose from 25.4% in 1966 to 31.6% in 1977 and again to 39.1% in 1989, but has since stabilized at 38.6% in 1997 (Rangan, 2000).

- Most US intrafirm exports are from US parents to their foreign affiliates, not from US affiliates to their foreign parents. Similarly, most US intrafirm imports are from foreign parents to their US affiliates. That is, the direction of intrafirm trade is primarily shipments from parents to their affiliates (Whichard & Lowe, 1998; Zeile, 1997).

- Nationality of the firm matters: intrafirm trade represents 70% of Canadian merchandise exports to the United States made by US-controlled firms and 80% of Canadian merchandise imports from the United States, compared to 25% and 17% for Canadian-controlled firms (Eden,1998).

- More than 90% of intrafirm exports by foreign parents to their US affiliates in the wholesale sector are finished goods for resale in the United States. Two-thirds of exports to manufacturing US affiliates, on the other hand, are unfinished so they face further processing in the United States (Eden, 1998; Zeile, 1997).

- The share of related party trade in total trade varies enormously by commodity, and differs between exports and imports (US Census, 2000). For example, the 1999 IFT shares of the top five leading US imports by value are: motor vehicles (82%), electrical machinery (63%), office machines and ADP equipment (68%), apparel and clothing (16%), petroleum (20%). The 1999 IFT shares of the top five leading US exports by value are: electric machinery, apparatus and appliances (44%), motor vehicles (60%), transport equipment (10%), office machines and ADP equipment (42%) and power generating machinery (37%).

- Most US-Canadian trade in business services is intrafirm (50% of Canadian exports, 60% of Canadian imports), and for certain components (e.g., automotive tooling charges) the share is close to 100 percent (Eden, 1998).

- In 1997, majority-owned foreign affiliates (MOFAs) represented 90% of all US foreign affiliates. MOFAs are reducing their reliance on internal production and using more unaffiliated suppliers, across all industries and all geographic areas (Mataloni, 1997).

- Overall, US international intrafirm trade is different from all US trade involving foreign MNEs (Zeile, 1997):

- *US intrafirm exports*: For US MNEs, most of the trade involves manufacturing affiliates and therefore is trade in intermediate goods. Exports from US parents tend to be automotive and machinery components, exported for further assembly. For foreign MNEs, most of the trade (2/3) involves wholesale affiliates and is therefore connected with distribution and marketing activities, and involves trade in finished goods (Zeile, 1997). Exports by wholesale trade affiliates from the US are mostly homogeneous commodities (food and crude materials), shipped by Japanese and French owned affiliates specializing in farm products. Therefore, US parents and foreign affiliates in the US tend to export very different types of intrafirm trade.

- *US intrafirm imports*: For US parents, intrafirm imports from their MOFAs now comes primarily (80%) from their manufacturing MOFAs. This is mostly trade in autos, and much of the trade is with Canada and Mexico under the Canada-US FTA and NAFTA. Machinery imports are also important. For US affiliates with foreign parents, US imports tend to be heterogeneous manufactured goods such as machinery or autos. A local presence is needed in the US to provide specialized after-sales service or to obtain continuous feedback from customers. So most US affiliates were set up to facilitate marketing of foreign made products (e.g., foreign cars). Three-quarters of all imports by these affiliates have been from their foreign parents.

Based on the above findings, we conclude that the pattern of international intrafirm trade between the United States and other countries appears to have somewhat different characteristics than international trade between unrelated parties. An important question for academics and policy makers, then, is how intrafirm trade changes our understanding and measures of traditional economic variables such as the balance of payments, national income, price indexes, industry location patterns? We begin to address this question by first examining the current international price program of the Bureau of Labor Statistics and how it handles intrafirm trade and transfer pricing.

THE BLS INTERNATIONAL PRICE PROGRAM (IPP)

Sources of US Trade Data

The US government produces three main types of international trade data, each of which requires US international price indexes for deflation, trends and forecasting purposes. First, the Bureau of the Census (BCEN) publishes the total dollar value of general exports and imports. Export figures are reported directly to BCEN; import figures come from the US Customs Service. Exports are defined as the physical movement of goods out of the United States, either through US territory, US dependencies (e.g., Puerto Rico), US customs bonded warehouses or US foreign trade zones. Exports are valued at the free-alongside-ship (f.a.s.) price in the foreign port, including all costs incurred to move the product to the point of exit (e.g., inland freight, insurance). Imports are defined as the physical movement of goods into the United States, in a manner analogous to exports. Imports are valued at the free-on-board (f.o.b.) price paid at the foreign port, excluding any additional costs (e.g., tariffs, insurance, international freight) to bring the product into the United States.

Second, the Bureau of Economic Analysis (BEA) produces US balance of payments account (BPA) data, including exports and imports of goods and services. Imports and exports are defined when ownership changes hands between a US resident and a foreign resident. The base for the BPA statistics is the BCEN trade volume figures, with minor adjustments.

Third, the Bureau of Economic Analysis produces National Income and Items Account

(NIPA) data for the US economy, showing the value and composition of national output and the distribution of income in the United States. The NIPA tables include US payments and receipts for foreign transactions; these statistics come from the BPA data with minor adjustments (e.g., Puerto Rico is part of the US BPA but not of the NIPA).

These different sources and types of international trade data, with their different purposes and uses, suggest that the Bureau of Labor Statistics must provide more than one international price index, and in fact, that is the case.

Purpose and Scope of the BLS International Price Program

The BLS International Price Program has published indexes of import and export prices for US merchandise trade and services since 1973. The "target universe" for the IPP includes all goods and services sold by the US residents to foreign buyers and purchased from abroad by US residents (BLS, 1997: 155).

The fundamental purpose behind the international price program is to answer the question "how will trade affect the production of goods and services in the economy?" (BLS, 1997: 154). In order to answer this question, real (constant dollar) measures for exports and imports are required. Given the difficulty of directly measuring and comparing quantities, the IPP proxies quantities by deflating the value of aggregate trade by price indexes. The value of import purchases is deflated by the import price index, the value of export sales by the export price index. Real net exports are measured by the gap between real exports and real imports:

$$\text{Real Net Exports} = X - M = \Sigma\, Px\, X\, /\, XPI - \Sigma\, Pm\, M\, /\, MPI \tag{1}$$

where X and M are the estimated aggregate quantities of exports and imports, $\Sigma\, Px\, X$ and $\Sigma\, Pm\, M$ the their current dollar values, XPI is the export price index and MPI the import price index.

The key functions of the BLS international price program are to (BLS, 1997: 158-9; 1999b):

- *Deflate trade statistics:* Deflate foreign trade and growth statistical series into real (constant dollar) terms. Deflated measures of international trade are needed in order to analyze trade movements and measure the impact of trade legislation. The IPP is primarily designed to deflate the US foreign trade statistics provided by the Bureau of the Census (BCEN) and the Bureau of Economic Analysis (BEA).

- *Measure inflation and price trends*: Measure short- and long-run trends in export and import prices and forecast future prices, at the national and industry levels, using the foreign trade statistics provided by BCEN and BEA.

There are other uses for the BLS international price indexes. Economists are interested in price and income *elasticities* in international trade, and movements in national *terms of trade* (the ratio of export prices to import prices). International price indexes can also be used to assess long-run *competitiveness* of particular US industries, relative to major trading partners. Exporters need to know how market prices are moving in countries to which they export if they wish to price to market; imports need to compare prices for imported products to domestically available goods in order to produce at minimum cost. International price indexes can be used in *contracts,* either in negotiations or in escalator clauses. Other uses include calculating *foreign currency price indexes*, the *pass through of exchange rate changes* into consumer prices, and *import prices by country of origin.*

Comparison with the Producer Price Index

We can think of the purposes for international price indexes as being either macro (at the national level) or micro (at the product level) in nature. This classification helps to distinguish the purpose of the IPP from the producer price index (PPI), which is also published by BLS. The PPI measures price changes in US total output, by industry, regardless of the destination of that output. Alterman (1997b: 19) compares the PPI to the international price program as follows:

The PPI program samples and estimates price changes across *industries* to produce net output indexes. Items produced and consumed within a given industry are *excluded* from the program's net output indexes....in the PPI, the same items from two different industries would show up in two *different* indexes. ..... The indexes produced by the BLS international price program are designed to construct the real net export component of the US National Income and Product Accounts, which are product-based as opposed to industry-based. Thus, the program samples and then estimates price change across *product* areas to produce import and export price indexes. The same items in two different industries would show up in the *same* index.

Table 1, which represents a modification of Alterman (1997b) to include the import price index, summarizes the key differences (for the purposes of this paper) between the IPP and the PPI. Thus, the PPI, with its focus on deflating industry-level output, has primarily meso (industry) and macro (national) purposes; whereas the IPP, with its focus on deflating internationally traded products, has primarily micro (product) and macro (national) purposes.

[Table 1 goes about here]

BLS Import and Export Price Definitions

The BLS defines *exports* as the value of physical movement of products (goods and services) out of a country, either from inside the country, bonded customs warehouses or foreign trade zones. Exports are valued as free alongside ship (f.a.s.); inland freight, insurance and other charges need to bring the product to the point of exit are included in the export price.

The BLS defines *imports* as the value of products of foreign origin, products of domestic origin returning to the exporting country unchanged, or products assembled overseas with components that originated inside the exporting country. There are two types of import prices, depending on where the product is in transit (BLS, 1999b).

A *general import* is measured when it passes into the importing country's customs territory, a customs bonded warehouse or a foreign trade zone (FTZ). Duties are deferred until the product leaves the warehouse and enters the importing country. General imports are valued at the free-on-board (f.o.b.) price at the foreign port; all duties, insurance and other costs levied to bring the product into the importing country are excluded, but costs to get the product to the point of export are included.

Imports for consumption are a second category of imports classified when the product passes out of a bonded warehouse or FTZ and into the importing country's territory. Since the primary difference between indirect entry through a bonded warehouse and direct sale to the importer is that customs duties are deferred until the product leaves the warehouse, this means that imports for consumption are measured inclusive of customs duties, whereas general imports are measured exclusive of customs duties.

When the purpose of an import price index is to deflate the trade statistics in order to measure the constant dollar (real) amount of imports, the BLS uses the general import price (i.e., the price exclusive of tariffs). When the purpose of the import price index is to measure the impact of imports on domestic inflation and short/long-term price trends, the BLS uses the import-for-consumption price index. The rationale is that the import price to the buyer, inclusive of all foreign costs (e.g., insurance, freight, foreign taxes) and importing country tariffs, but before any domestic costs (e.g., in-land freight) are added, better represents the price to the consumer and thus the inflationary potential of imported products.

Intrafirm Trade, Transfer Pricing and the IPP[1]

Before 1994, the BLS only collected information on prices for transactions between related parties that were considered to be at arm's length (that is, they trended with market prices). All other transfer prices were considered out of scope and discarded. Starting in 1994, the Bureau began collecting pricing information for all intrafirm transactions but continued to exclude from index estimation all transfer prices that were not market based.

This procedure created several problems. Given that intrafirm trade represents close to 50% of US imports and one-third of exports, the exclusion of non-market-based transfer prices meant that some fraction, potentially very large, of US international trade was being omitted from the international price program. Since most intrafirm trade is conducted through large multinational enterprises, the procedure also biased the indexes towards pricing of small, domestic firms. The extent and direction of the biases was unknown.

In 1997, the BLS conducted a study comparing the current price indexes with indexes that included all transfer prices regardless of whether they trended with the market. Based on this study, the BLS revised its procedure and began to use all transfer prices in the IPP starting with the February 1998 index. The full impact of this sampling change should only now be visible in the export and import price indexes since it takes two to three years for any change in sampling technique to be fully reflected, due to the rolling nature of the sampling process (BLS, 1997, 1999b).

The most recent change occurred in June 1998 when the BLS replaced the "market trending" versus "non-market trending" categories in the survey with five categories designed to capture the type of transfer pricing method: market based pricing, cost based pricing, no intra-company transfer, other non-market based pricing and pricing method unknown.

Constructing the BLS International Price Indexes

The BLS uses fixed-quantity Laspeyres import and export price indexes, which measure price changes by fixing quantities at their reference or base period values. The general formula for the international price indexes is:

$$L_P = \Sigma \, p_t \, q_{t-1} \, / \, \Sigma \, p_{t-1} \, q_{t-1} = \Sigma \, (\, p_t \, / \, p_{t-1} \,) \, s_{t-1} \tag{2}$$

where L_p is the Laspeyres index, p_t the price in period t, and s_{t-1} the fixed weight in period t-1 which can be either a fixed quantity or sales share.

The BLS constructs the international price indexes in stages, with the index number for a basic aggregate constructed first (the classification or weight group in the IPP) and then the basic units aggregated together across firms based on trade value weights.[2] The BLS also produces a chained Laspeyres price index, a sequence of price indexes, measuring the price changes of products between a fixed base period and the current time period for any given month, using the following chain formula for index I:

$$I_{t, \, t+2} = I_{t, \, t+1} \, \times \, I_{t+1, \, t+2} \tag{3}$$

The main feature of the fixed quantity Laspeyres index formula is the use of fixed reference-period quantities applied to aggregate prices. A fixed-quantity index has certain advantages. First, the true rate of price change will be at least as great as that computed by fixed-quantity index (BLS, 1999a). Second, the fixed-quantity Laspeyres index formula is also consistent in aggregation; that is, the value of the index calculated in two stages is equal to the value of the index calculated in a single stage.

One problem is that substitution among products in response to a price change, either by consumers or producers, is not taken into account. In addition, the index assumes that quality is fixed and new goods do not appear. These are typical problems in a domestic-based Laspeyres fixed-weight index (BLS, 1999a).

These problems should be even more prominent in international trade since more than one country is involved. In a closed economy, if the relative price of product X increases, consumers will substitute away from that product. In an open economy, importers have the additional choice of being able to switch to cheaper foreign substitutes, causing a switch in the country of origin for the product. New products and quality changes can also cause overall trade patterns to shift. For example, when a price increase occurs simultaneously with a quality improvement, the price increase will be overstated unless a quality adjustment is made. In addition, the market basket has changed since the items are no longer identical. The BLS addresses this problem by changing the base-period weights through frequent resampling of firms and updating of trade weights. Updating procedures transform a fixed-weight index into a chain index. One potential problem with chain indexes, however, is that chaining may cause the index to drift and introduce measurement error.

In the next section, we use simple examples to outline and evaluate the range of prices that could be used by a statistical agency to calculate export and import price indexes. We compare this list to those currently used by the Bureau of Labor Statistics.

PRICE INDEXES AND THE INTERNATIONAL TRANSPORTATION CHAIN
The International Transportation Chain: Getting from Here to There
One of the critical questions that must be answered before one can start to construct international price indexes is "which price should be measured?" Since there are multiple "slips

between the cup and the lip", that is, from the original point of origin to the final destination point, determining at which point to measure export and import prices is a critical first step. It may also be that the "right" point depends on the purpose for the index; different purposes may lead to the selection of different price indexes.

Figure 1 illustrates the process by which a good is produced in one country and exported to a second country. We can think of the whole sequence as an *international transportation chain*, the chain of prices that emerge as an exported product moves from production in the origin country to final sales in the destination country.

[Figure 1 goes here]

In Figure 1, the final point where value is added before export is point A (the factory gate). From there, the product moves to point B, normally a bonded warehouse, trading company or foreign trade zone. Inland freight and insurance costs are incurred as the product moves from the factory gate to the warehouse or FTZ. When the product moves out the exit point export taxes are added (subsidies deducted) and domestic value added taxes are deducted. This point (point C) represents the water's edge point for the exporting country. The product price at this point has two names: from the exporter's perspective it is the free-alongside-ship (f.a.s.) export price; from the importer's perspective, the free-on-board (f.o.b.) import price. Crossborder transport costs are then added to move the product to the water's edge point of entry (point D) for the importing country. The product enters the importing country normally through a commission agent, bonded warehouse or foreign trade zone. At the water's edge entry point, cross-border insurance and freight have been added; the price is now inclusive of cost, insurance and freight -- the c.i.f. import price. Once the product moves out of the warehouse or FTZ, customs duties and any value added taxes are levied on the importer (point E). The product is then sold to a distributor, another firm for further processing, or to a final consumer (point F), where additional taxes such as sales taxes may be due.

The transportation chain therefore stretches from points A to F and involves several different prices along the way. What does this transportation chain imply for the possible selection of import and export prices? We first examine the price indexes as defined by the BLS, and then focus on other possible indexes.

The International Transportation Chain: A Numerical Example

A numerical example of the international transportation chain may be helpful here; see Table 2 below. Table 2 illustrates how the price changes as a product (computer keyboards) moves from a Taiwanese manufacturer (Acer) to a US distributor (e.g., Wal-Mart) and then to US retail consumers. Acer's price consists of standard cost plus a gross profit mark-up of 20%. There are in-land transport costs (freight, insurance and any fees) to be paid in each country, along with cross-border transport costs. Assume that Taiwan levies a 25% export tax and the US a 10% tariff.[3] Lastly, assume Wal-Mart makes a 10% gross profit margin based on the US retail price. Location points in Table 2 refer specific location points in Figure 1.

[Table 2 goes here]

Figure 2 provides an alternative conception of the transportation chain linking factor gate to retail price, using Michael Porter's value chain of primary activities to show how price changes as the product moves from the factory gate in the exporting country to the final retail consumer in the importing country. The numbers in this figure are based on Table 2 and can also be directly linked to Figure 1. The general export price (f.a.s.) and the general import price (f.o.b.), which are the key prices in the BLS international price program, are highlighted in bold in Figure

2.

[Figure 2 goes here]

Alternative Price Indexes along the Transportation Chain

Figures 1 and 2 and Table 2 suggest that there are several different ways to measure the impact of international trade prices on a domestic economy, in addition to the general export (f.a.s.) and general import (f.o.b.) prices. Let us look at the alternatives.

The *factory gate price* in the exporting country (point A in Figure 1) measures the private sector product price before the decision is made to export or sell the product locally.

The *pre-tax export price* measures the private sector product price (factory gate plus inland transport, insurance and fees), which is the real cost of resources used by the exporting country to produce the product. This is point B in Figure 1, where the product moves from the factory gate into the warehouse or FTZ. The pre-tax export price measures the economic cost incurred by putting resources into producing this product rather than some other product. Government export taxes are ignored, as are international transport charges. Increased production costs raise the pre-tax export price, but higher export taxes do not affect this price (unlike the general export price which includes export taxes). From the perspective of the exporting country, the pre-tax export price represents the true opportunity cost to producers of exports in terms of forgone domestic consumption.

The *post-tax or water's edge export price* measures the price as the product moves offshore; i.e., inclusive of export taxes (subsidies) and exclusive of domestic value added taxes. The water's edge export price is the key price used by the BLS in constructing the export price index for purposes of deflating US Balance of Payments export statistics in order to measure the constant dollar (real) value of US exports.[4] This price, the general export price (f.a.s.), is shown

16

as point C in Figure 1 or as $100 in Table 2 and Figure 2. The BLS also considers this price, from the importing country's perspective, to be the general import price (f.o.b.), and uses this price index to deflate US Balance of Payments import statistics in order to measure the constant dollar amount of US imports.

The *pre-tariff or water's edge import price (c.i.f.)* is the price of delivering a product to the importing country's point of entry or water's edge. This is point D in Figure 1. The c.i.f. price includes international freight and insurance but excludes tariffs and any domestic value added taxes. As international transport costs change between locations and methods of transport, this price would move separately from the pre-tax export price. From the perspective of the exporting country, this is the price for moving the exported product to importing country's border.

The *post-tariff import price (c.i.f.)* is the price of delivering a product to the importer, inclusive of the customs duty. This is point E in Figure 1. Since duties vary between countries, this price provides a measure of the cost of getting the product "on the ground" ("over the tariff wall") in the importing country. The Bureau of Labor Statistics calls this the import-for-consumption price, and uses this price index to calculate the impact of imports on domestic inflation and short/long-term price trends.

In a free trade area, such as the NAFTA, where tariffs are zero between member countries the pre-tariff and post-tariff import prices should be the same. For all other cases, the two indexes will differ depending on the effective tariff rate. For example, it is well known that every quota has a tariff equivalent, and that tariff-cum-quotas can be converted to effective tariff rates. Where the importing country sets different tariff rates (e.g., FTA, MFN, General) and/or nontariff barriers across countries, two exporters with the same water's edge import price will have different post-tariff import prices.

The *retail price* is the price paid by the final consumer in the importing country (point F in Figure 1), inclusive of all taxes, insurance and freight costs and commissions along the transportation chain. For the exporter, this price is the appropriate one for competitiveness comparisons with domestic producers and other foreign countries' exporters in the importing country's market. The higher is the exporter's final retail price relative to other firms' retail prices, the less competitive it is relative to other firms in the eyes of consumers in the importing country. In effect, this is the "bottom line" price where the "rubber meets the road".

Implications for the BLS International Price Program

Our transportation chain analysis has one clear implication: <u>different public policy goals require different price indexes.</u>

First, if the goal is to deflate Balance of Payments statistics for international trade, the current policy of the BLS -- the general export price (f.a.s.) and general import price (f.o.b.) -- is probably the correct one. These price indexes measure the terms of trade facing the United States in international markets.

Second, if the goal is to assess export competitiveness, two different prices emerge depending on whether one takes an "export neutrality" or "import neutrality" perspective.[5] From the viewpoint of producers in the exporting country, they need to compare the real resource costs of two alternatives: exports and domestic sales. This suggests the appropriate "export neutrality" price index should be based on the pre-tax export price (point B in Figure 1) not the general export price (f.a.s.).

On the other hand, for comparisons between exporters from different countries, the appropriate "import neutrality" price index should be based on the water's edge import price (point D). The potential differences between the water's edge import price and the post-tariff import price (point E) suggests that point D would be a better choice because it is not affected by cases where the importing country sets different tariff rates for different countries or by movements in trade tax rates over time. This price might also be the appropriate one for measuring exchange rate pass through effects.

Third, when calculating the impact of imports on domestic inflation and price trends, the water's edge import price (point D) might be superior to the post-tariff import price (point E) because it is not affected by differences in tariffs and NTBs levied across countries, or changes in these rates over time.

This analysis suggests that the BLS might want to track two export prices that are currently not being tracked (points B and D) if competitiveness of US exports is an important issue, and substitute a different import price (point D) for the current import-for-consumption price (point E) used to calculate inflation measures.

In none of the above analysis have we discussed the impact of *ownership* on export and import prices. We turn now to modeling the differences between international interfirm trade (trade between unrelated parties) and intrafirm trade (trade between related parties).

THE THEORY OF INTERNATIONAL INTRAFIRM TRADE

The MNE's Optimal Transfer Pricing Policies

In this section, we begin to address the implications of international intrafirm trade and transfer pricing for the BLS international price indexes. We start first by comparing international trade between unrelated parties with trade between MNE affiliates. Our purpose is to develop a theory of the MNE's optimal resource allocation (output, sales, international trade) and pricing decisions for international intrafirm trade in tangible products.[6]

Arm's Length Trade between Unrelated Parties

Assume the MNE consists of two unrelated firms, a foreign firm (F) and a US firm (U). Assume that firm F ships an intermediate good to the US firm for finishing and final sale in the US market. Firm F also sells the same intermediate good to arm's length parties at price p^e in its domestic market. Let Q_i be domestic output, Y_i domestic sales, $R_i(Y_i)$ total revenue from Y_i and $C_i(Q_i)$ total cost of Q_i, where $i = F, U$. Let X be the volume of trade and p the price of X so that the value of international trade is $p X$.[7] We assume, for simplicity, that one unit of X is required to make one unit of Q_U so that $Q_U = Y_U = X$.

We assume transactions costs of search, monitoring and enforcement of contracts must be incurred in private markets between unrelated firms, particularly where markets are characterized by uncertainty. We also assume that transactions costs are higher in international markets than in domestic markets. Without loss of generality, we model only the transactions costs of international trade, ignoring the smaller costs of domestic trade.[8] We model these costs as $T = \beta_i X$, where $i = F, U$, assuming that transactions costs are positively related to the volume of trade. The profit functions of the two firms are:

$$\pi_F = R_F(Y_F) + (p - \beta_F) X - C_F(Q_F) \tag{4}$$

$$\pi_U = R_U(Y_U) - C_U(Q_U) - (p + \beta_U) X = R_U(X) - C_U(X) - (p + \beta_U) X \tag{5}$$

Since each firm individually maximizes its profits, the first order conditions for a profit maximum are:

$$p - \beta_F = MR_F = MC_F \tag{6}$$

$$p + \beta_U = MR_U - MC_U = NMR_U \qquad (7)$$

where NMR_U is the net marginal revenue from US sales of the finished good.[9] Solving for p, equations (6,7) can be usefully rewritten as:

$$p = MC_x{}^F + \beta_F = NMR_x{}^U - \beta_U \qquad (8)$$

where $MC_x{}^F$ is the marginal cost of the exporter firm and $NMR_x{}^U$ is the net marginal revenue of the importer firm. That is, the equilibrium (negotiated) arm's length price equates the marginal cost of exports to the net marginal revenue from imports, including international transactions costs. This is illustrated in Figure 3.

[Figure 3 goes here]

Figure 3 shows that two unrelated firms, each faced by transactions costs in international trade, will negotiate an arm's length price of p_0 at point a with the volume of trade X_0. The effective return to the exporter, firm F, is $p_0 - \beta_F$; the effective cost for the importer firm is $p_0 + \beta_U$. Total transactions costs are the distance bc times X_0.

Intrafirm Trade between Related Parties

Now let us assume that the firms are related parties so that X represents intrafirm trade and p the transfer price. Let firm F be the parent firm, shipping the intermediate good X to its US subsidiary for finishing and final sale in the US market. Because the firms are related parties, the transactions costs of international trade are reduced. Without loss of generality, we assume them to be zero. Then the pre-tax global profit of the MNE, B, is:

$$\pi = [R_F(Y_F) + p X - C_F(Q_F)] + [R_U(X) - C_U(X) - p X] \qquad (9)$$

where the first bracket is the parent's profit and the second bracket, the US subsidiary's profit.

Because the two affiliates are related, the multinational enterprise (MNE) maximizes the joint profits of the two affiliates. In the absence of profit taxes and tariffs, the first order condition for a global profit maximum is:

$$MR_F = MC_F = NMR_U = \lambda \qquad (10)$$

with the shadow price of intrafirm trade, λ, being the marginal cost of the exporter affiliate. As is well known, the nominal (or money) transfer price $\mathbf{p}$ disappears when joint MNE profits are maximized (Horst 1971; Diewert 1985; Eden 1985). However, there is still an efficient transfer price based on the shadow price of intrafirm trade. We can usefully rewrite equation (10) in short form as:

$$MC_x^F = NMR_x^U = \lambda \qquad (11)$$

which says that the marginal cost to the exporter (the foreign parent) should equal the net marginal revenue earned by the importer (the US affiliate) from intrafirm trade. Thus, the efficient transfer price λ equals MC_x^F.

Figure 3 provides an illustration of the impact of moving from trade between two unrelated parties, faced with transactions costs, to trade between related parties without transactions costs. The new equilibrium is point d with a larger volume of trade X_{MNE}. The transfer price $\mathbf{p_{MNE}}$, however, may be larger or smaller than $\mathbf{p_0}$ depending on the incidence of transactions costs on the two private firms.

What is clear is that national welfare is unambiguously higher. When trade occurs between unrelated firms, the national welfare gain is measured by triangle eaf. When trade occurs between related parties, national welfare is measured by the much larger area, triangle gd0. The difference is the impact of international transactions costs, which deter international trade and are a nonproductive use of resources.

The Impact of An External Market Price

Suppose the exporting firm can sell as much as it wants at the domestic external market price p^e. How does this affect our analysis? Hirshleifer (1956, 1957) proved that, in the absence of interdependencies of demand or supply between the related parties, the MNE will choose to buy or sell at the external market price. Thus, the *external market price* becomes the efficient transfer price for the MNE because the external price represents the opportunity cost of the *internal market (the hierarchy)*. To quote Diewert (1985: 47):

> If there is a well defined external market for the good where units can be bought
>
> and sold at a common price w, then there is no transfer pricing problem: the firm
>
> should value the intermediate good at price w in both plants.

We can easily prove the Hirshleifer Rule by modifying equation (9), the MNE's objective function as follows:

$$\pi = [R_F (Y_F) + p^e S + p X - C_F (Q_F)] + [R_U (X) - C_U (X) - p X] \qquad (12)$$

where $Q_F = X + S + Y_F$. The first order condition for a profit maximum becomes:

$$MC_X^F = NMR_X^U = p^e = \lambda \qquad (13)$$

This is illustrated in Figure 4 for the case where the external market price p^e lies above the initial transfer price p_0 so the exporting firm reduces its intrafirm exports from X_0 to X_1, selling S on the open market.[10] While the importer's profits are reduced by this action (from the area dap_1 to dce), the exporter's profits increase sufficiently (from area $0ap_0$ to 0be) that total MNE profits rise by the triangle abc. Thus, valuing intrafirm trade at the arm's length external market price – the *comparable uncontrolled price (CUP)* - is efficiency (and profit) maximizing for the MNE.

[Figure 4 goes here]

However, Hirshleifer's Rule does not hold where interdependencies in demand or supply exist between affiliates of the MNE that do not exist between unrelated firms.[11] Just as we showed above in Figure 1 that unrelated firms face transactions costs that are not borne by related firms, which make the arm's length price not equivalent to the related party price, so can interdependencies make a comparison of the two prices inappropriate and misleading. For example, where related parties can operate with a more efficient technology or achieve additional economies of scope compared to unrelated parties, we expect the efficient transfer price to lie below the arm's length price.

Colbert & Spicer (1995) provide one test of this hypothesis, examining transfer pricing policies in the US electronics industry between upstream component producers and downstream assemblers. Where asset specificity is high for either the upstream or downstream affiliate, they found that the MNE substitutes cost-based for market-based prices. Similarly, cost-based prices were more likely to be used where state-of-the-art processes were involved; while market-based prices were used for products using mature process technologies. The parent firm was also less willing to allow either division to buy/sell on the outside market where asset specificity created strong interdependencies between the buying and selling divisions. We infer, therefore, that MNEs using cost-based transfer pricing methods, rather than market-based methods, for particular types of intrafirm transactions are simply recognizing and adapting to interdependencies that render the Hirshleifer Rule inappropriate.

The Impact of Taxes and Tariffs

We now turn to the impact of government regulations on the MNE's transfer price. Assume that the US and foreign governments tax the MNE's profits at rate t_i where t_F is less than t_U,[12] and that the US government also levies a customs duty at rate ϑ on imports. Then B*, the after-tax global profit of the MNE, is:

$$\pi^* = (1 - t_F) [R_F (Y_F) + p X - C_F (Q_F)] + (1 - t_U) [R_U (Y_U) - C_U (Q_U) - (1 + \vartheta) p X] \quad (14)$$

where we assume, as before, that $Q_U = X$. Differentiating (14) with respect to Q_i, Y_i and X, the first order condition is:

$$(1 - t_F) MC_x^F = (1 - t_U) NMR_x^U + [(t_U - t_F) - \tau] p \quad (15)$$

Equation (15) says that the MNE should equate the after-tax marginal cost of the foreign parent exporter to the after-tax net marginal revenue of the US importer, adjusted for the tax differential minus the tariff times the transfer price. Because we have assumed $t_U > t_F$, the foreign parent would prefer to overinvoice its exports to its US affiliate in order to shift the profits to the home country; however, the tariff acts in the opposite direction to encourage underinvoicing of intrafirm imports. Which effect is stronger depends on the tax gap relative to the tariff rate. We can see this by differentiating equation (14) with respect to p and using the envelope theorem:

$$\partial \pi^* / \partial p = ((1 - t_F) - (1 - t_U) (1 + \tau)) X = [(t_U - t_F) - \tau (1 - t_U)] X$$

$$= (1 - t_U) [\{(t_U - t_F)/(1 - t_U)\} - \tau] X$$

$$> 0 \text{ if } (t_U - t_F)/(1 - t_U) > \tau \text{, and vice versa if } < \tau \quad (16)$$

which is the well-known result (Horst, 1971; Eden, 1995, 1998) that the MNE's optimal transfer pricing policy depends on the relative tax differential compared to the *ad valorem* tariff. If the tax differential dominates, the MNE will overinvoice the imports in order to shift profits out of the United States; if the tariff dominates, the MNE will reverse its pricing policy and underinvoice the imports.

Equation (16) shows that the Hirshleifer Rule will not be followed by the MNE when government barriers such as tariffs and corporate income tax differentials impede intrafirm trade flows. Thus, the profit maximizing transfer price in the presence of taxes and/or tariffs -- let us call it **p*** -- will equal neither the shadow price λ nor the external market price **p^e**.

There is strong evidence in previous studies (Eden, 1998, Ch. 7; Hines, 1998) that MNEs do engage in transfer price manipulation when faced by tax and trade barriers.[13] For this reason, both corporate income tax and customs authorities have developed government regulations designed to discourage such manipulation. We can model this regulation by assuming the government imposes a transfer pricing ceiling if ∂ B*\∂ **p** is positive (and floor if negative), which we can call the regulated transfer price **W**.[14] The MNE is therefore forced to set its profit maximizing transfer price equal to the regulated price **W**, for tax and/or tariff purposes.

The existence of a regulated transfer price raises the question as to whether the MNE keeps two sets of books; one set of external books for the regulator (using transfer price **W**) and a separate set of books of internal books (using **p***). Most evidence suggests that, at least for merchandise trade flows, MNEs do not keep two sets of books, which means that **p*** should equal **W** (Eden, 1998: 295-99). The contemporaneous documentation requirements and inaccuracy penalty tax introduced as part of the 1994 overhaul of IRC section 482 (the transfer pricing provisions in the US corporate income tax code) also strongly suggest that **p*** should equal **W** (Eden, 1998).

Table 3 summarizes the results of this section, outlining the different transfer prices that will be chosen by the MNE depending on whether (i) tariffs or taxes are imposed on intrafirm trade, (ii) external market prices are available, and (iii) interdependencies in supply and/or demand affect MNE behavior.

[Table 3 goes here]

Implications for the BLS International Price Program

In this section, we explore some implications for the BLS international price program (IPP) that emerge from our theory of MNE intrafirm trade and transfer pricing.

Should Intrafirm Trade Be Included in the BLS International Price Program?

On both theoretical and practical grounds, the clear answer is yes. International intrafirm trade, even where transfer prices diverge from market-based prices, belongs in the IPP. On theoretical grounds, MNEs determine the optimal volume of intrafirm trade in the same manner as private firms, that is, comparing the private costs and benefits of trade relative to domestic sales and production. While there are differences, most notably that (i) related party firms maximize joint rather than individual profits, (ii) face lower transactions costs than trade between unrelated firms, and (iii) may benefit from interdependencies in demand and supply, this does not affect the bottom line argument that intrafirm trade flows respond to economic incentives and costs in a similar manner to trade between unrelated parties.

On practical grounds, if the key purpose of the program is to deflate US international trade figures, since almost half of US trade is conducted by multinational enterprises, perhaps half of that trade is intrafirm in nature and MNEs tend to be much larger than domestic firms, leaving intrafirm trade out of the international price index calculations will omit large amounts of trade from the indexes and should clearly skew the indexes towards small exporters and importers.

What Is the Appropriate Transfer Price?

In theory, the appropriate transfer price for constructing international price indexes should be the profit-maximizing transfer price p^* set by the multinational enterprise. However, as Table

3 shows, the profit maximizing price will vary depending on the presence or absence of (1) external markets, (2) interdependencies within the MNE group, (3) taxes and tariffs and (4) transfer pricing legislation that forces the MNE to use the regulated price **W**. In the United States, transfer prices are regulated under both the corporate income tax and customs duty codes so that regulated prices **W** do exist (although they may differ between customs and tax, we discuss this below). This suggests that the appropriate transfer prices to be used, in theory, are the regulated prices set either by US Customs or by the Internal Revenue Service. Which pricing program is more appropriate for BLS purposes depends on practical considerations, which are addressed later in the paper.

Should Transfer Prices that Are Not Market Based Be Omitted from the IPP?

While the BLS collects data on intrafirm trade, asking respondents to flag the type of transfer pricing method used as one of five possibilities (market based, cost based, other non-market based, pricing method unknown, no intrafirm transaction), until February 1998 the IPP only included intrafirm trade where the firms have tagged "market based" as the transfer pricing method. Thus, the BLS before February 1998 omitted cost-based and other non-market based transfer prices from the international price indexes.

On the surface, this made intuitive sense: cost-based prices do not reflect market forces. If international price indexes are to be useful, they should reflect prices in the market place. However, we argue that *all* transfer prices, regardless of the method used for computing the price, should be used in the construction of the IPP as long as these are the prices actually paid in international transactions between related parties.

First, as we have seen above, the MNE will choose on its own, in the absence of government barriers and interdependencies among its affiliates, to use prices of comparable products in the external market place as the efficient transfer price. This is the Hirshleifer Rule. Where interdependencies do exist, however, other pricing methods may be more efficient. For example, as Colbert & Spicer (1995) show, where asset specificity is high for either the upstream or downstream divisions, the MNE will prefer to use cost-based transfer prices and discourage the affiliates from engaging in trade in external markets. Therefore ignoring cost-based prices means that the BLS international price indexes are not incorporating the actual price paid or payable for international transactions.

Second, government transfer pricing regulations (as we show below) require MNEs to use market-based prices only where comparable external market prices exist. In other cases, cost-based prices that build up from the manufacturer's price are commonly accepted as legitimate transfer pricing policies.

What about the case raised in Alterman (1997a) where in 1997 the transfer prices for exports of dies and wafers, and for imports of semiconductor chips, were based on costs and therefore moved very slowly, while the producer and consumer prices fell over the same period? Some economists questioned whether the export price index might be inaccurate. As we have argued above, however, it would not be unusual, particularly in industries characterized by large economies of scale and new technology, for MNEs to use cost-based transfer prices. Therefore, one should expect differences in movements between international prices (based on costs) and domestic prices (based on market prices) in industries such as semiconductors. The bottom line is that all transfer prices should be included. Where such prices differ from final consumer prices, an explanation should be provided rather than drop the transfer prices from the IPP.

GOVERNMENT TRANSFER PRICING REGULATIONS

The Arm's Length Standard

In the United States, two different organizations are responsible for policing the MNE's transfer prices. US Customs uses the GATT Customs Valuation Code (CVC), under Section 1401 of the US Customs Act, to regulate transfer prices; the Internal Revenue Service (IRS) follows the OECD transfer pricing guidelines (OECD 1995) under Section 482 of the US Internal Revenue Code. While the terminology is quite different between the two organizations (customs and tax), the underlying principle -- the *arm's length standard* -- is the same: two related parties should set the same transfer price for an intrafirm transaction as two unrelated parties would have set if they had been engaged in the same or similar transaction under the same or similar circumstances.

The arm's length standard asks the question: What would the negotiated price for the transaction have been if the parties had not been related to one another? Clearly, the answer to this question must be hypothetical since the firms are related parties. Two possible approaches to answering the question are the following:

- The price set by one of the related parties in a comparable transaction under comparable circumstances with an unrelated party is used as an estimate for the transfer price. Where the MNE either buys outside or sells outside, under comparable circumstances, the price negotiated with one or more unrelated parties (called an *internal* comparable) can be used as the arm's length price.

- The price negotiated between two or more unrelated parties engaged in the same or similar transactions under the same or similar circumstances is used as an estimate for the transfer price, adjusted if necessary to improve comparability. This approach is called an *external comparable.*

Both the internal and external comparable approaches have a strong theoretical economic foundation in the Hirshleifer Rule: where an external market price exists, the MNE's efficient transfer price should be the external market price. Thus, government regulation based on comparable prices in the external market place is theoretically sound.

Two caveats are key here however. First, MNEs are *integrated businesses*; affiliates are under common control, with common goals (maximizing *joint* not individual profits) and common resources. This means that interdependencies in demand and/or supply are likely to characterize intrafirm trade. In such cases, the Hirshleifer Rule breaks down and the external market price is not the efficient transfer price. Whether the efficient price lies above or below the external price depends on the nature of the interdependencies. For example, if the MNE enjoys large economies of scale and scope in its international operations, transfer prices may lie below external market prices. If external markets have transactions costs that are not faced by related party trade, the arm's length price must take these differences in transactions costs into account.

The second caveat is that the key to determining the appropriate arm's length price is *comparability* of the related party and independent transactions. Any differences in product or functional comparability (functions performed, resources used, risks assumed) must be taken into account if the internal or external comparable methods are to be good proxies for the arm's length transfer price.

Transfer Pricing Regulation by the Internal Revenue Service (IRS)

Transfer pricing regulations under Section 482 of the US Internal Revenue Code (IRC) follow the arm's length standard, which was first developed in the United States and then adopted by the OECD (Eden 1998; forthcoming). The OECD transfer pricing guidelines OECD (1995) and IRC Section 482 outline three general approaches to regulating the MNE's transfer prices for purposes of determining taxation of MNE profits under the corporate income tax.[15]

Product Comparable Methods

The method most closely related to the arm's length standard is the *comparable uncontrolled price (CUP) method* because it focuses specifically on the price of the product of the transaction in question. Two types of CUPs are possible: *an external CUP* (the price set between two unrelated parties for the same or similar product sold under the same or similar circumstances) and an *internal CUP* (where the MNE simultaneously sells/buys the same or similar product under the same or similar circumstances with an affiliate and an unrelated party. An advantage of a product comparable method is that it focuses directly on both parties to the transaction (i.e., it is a two-sided method) and the price they negotiate for the particular product; thus CUP most closely proxies for the arm's length standard.

Functional Comparable Methods

Where it is not possible to find an internal or external CUP, the next best approach is to look for a functional comparable, that is, for unrelated firms that perform the same or similar functions under the same or similar circumstances as the related party. In this case, the tax or tariff authority picks one of the two related parties (normally the one with the simplest functions and no valuable intangibles) as the tested party, and looks for comparable firms that could provide the same functions. Because functional comparable methods focus on one party to the transaction, they are considered one-sided methods, one step removed from the ideal approach ("one slip between the CUP and the lip"). As a result, measurement error is more likely with functional comparables than with product comparable methods. On the other hand, where external markets do not exist or are plagued by imperfections, it may be impossible to use the CUP method, functional comparables may be the most feasible alternative.

There are two types of functional comparables depending on which party is selected as the tested party:

- If the chosen firm is the exporter (manufacturer), the government estimates the normal gross profit markup earned by unrelated manufacturers performing the same or similar functions as the related party (commonly known as *contract manufacturers)* and adds this gross return to the standard average cost of the related party to determine the transfer price. This is called the *cost plus (C+) method*.

- If the chosen firm is the importer (distributor), the government estimates the normal gross profit margin earned by unrelated distributors performing the same or similar functions to the related party (*contract distributors*) and subtracts this gross return from the retail price to find the transfer price. This method is called the *resale price (RP) method*.

Profit Comparable Methods

A third set of transfer pricing methods applicable to the corporate income tax focus, not on product nor on functional comparables, but on profit-based comparables. There are no equivalents to these methods under the GATT code. There are two general types of profit comparables:

- The *comparable profit method (CPM)* assumes that the related party (normally the firm with the simpler functions and no valuable intangibles) should earn the same normal net return as firms in the same industry, selling the same or similar products under the same or similar circumstances.[16] A common measure of the net profit return is the return on employed capital (the ratio of operating income to operating capital). Where the unrelated firms earn a range of returns, the related party's profit level is expected to fall within this range; if it falls outside, the related party's profit level is normally adjusted to the median of the interquartile (25%-75%) range. The transfer price is determined by backwards calculation from the net profit margin/markup. CPM is two steps removed from the ideal transfer pricing method (two "slips between the CUP and the lip"). First, CPM is a one-sided method like the functional comparables. Second, because CPM focuses on net profits, not on gross margins/markups, it introduces a second element of uncertainty and therefore an additional source of measurement error.

- *Profit split method*. Net profit on the transaction is split between the two related parties based on their relative responsibilities, assumption of risks and capital contributions. This method has the advantage that it is two-sided since both parties are taken into account. However, it is primarily an inward looking method, which tends to lead to simple profit splits in practice (e.g., 50-50 or shares in proportion to capital contributions) that introduce measurement error.

The US Customs Transfer Pricing Program

In the 1970s, US Customs used to apply nine separate methods to value imports, including several designed to raise tariff revenues and offer protection to local firms. Since the Tokyo Customs Valuation Code was introduced into U.S. customs law in 1980 as U.S. Customs Code section 1401, the nine methods have been reduced to four, in descending order of priority: (i) transaction value, (ii) deductive value (similar to the resale price method), (iii) computed value (similar to the cost plus method), and (iv) derived value ("any other method").

Transactions Value Method (TV)

The US Customs under section 1401 of the US Customs Act defines *transactions value (TV)* as the price actually paid or payable for a product when it is sold for to the United States, plus the following items with respect to the imported merchandise, but only if these amounts are not otherwise included in the price actually paid or payable and there is sufficient information to warrant their inclusion:

- packing costs incurred by the US importer;

- any selling commissions incurred by the US importer;

- the value, where appropriate, of any assist;

- any royalty or license fee that the buyer is required to pay, directly or indirectly, as a condition of the sale of the imported merchandise for export to the United States; and

- the proceeds of any subsequent resale, disposal or use of the imported merchandise that accrue, directly or indirectly, to the seller.

If sufficient information is not available, for any reason, with respect to any amount in (i) through (v), the transactions value cannot be determined using this approach. In such cases, TV may be determined using the price of identical or similar merchandise exported to the United States at the same commercial level in substantially the same quantities at or about the same time, as that merchandise being appraised. Where differences in commercial level or quantities occur, adjustments must be made for these differences based on sufficient information. If two or more transactions values are determined, the appraised value[17] must be based on the lower of the two transaction values.

The transaction value of imported merchandise shall be the appraised value only if: (i) the buyer and seller are not related [18]; (ii) the parties are related but the relationship did not influence the price actually paid or payable, or (iii) the TV closely approximates the transactions value, deductive value or computed value for identical or similar merchandise exported to the US about the same time as the imported merchandise and sold to unrelated buyers in the United States. Any differences in commercial levels, quantities, costs, commissions, and costs incurred between unrelated buyers that are not incurred between the related parties should be taken into account in computing (iii).

In determining transaction value, the "price actually paid or payable" does not depend on its method of derivation or how payment is made. The word "payable" refers to a situation in which the price has been agreed upon, but actual payment has not been made at the time of importation. The price may be the result of discounts, increases, negotiations or the application of a formula (e.g., the LME price in effect on the date of export). Payment may be made by letters of credit or negotiable instruments and may be made directly or indirectly. However, any change in the price actually paid or payable that occurs between the buyer and seller after the date of importation of the merchandise into the United States must be disregarded in determining the transaction value.

The GATT code allows each country to choose whether or not to include or exclude from the customs value (i) transport costs to the place of importation, (ii) loading, unloading and handling charges associated with transport to the place of importation, and (iii) the cost of insurance. The GATT code is explicit that the customs valuation should not include any duties and taxes levied by the importing country, provided that these taxes can be distinguished from the price actually paid or payable for the imported goods.

The US government has chosen to exclude these items from the customs value so that "price actually paid or payable" means the total price *excluding* any and all costs related to international shipment from the country of exportation to the place of importation in the United States. Thus, transactions value in the United States is equivalent to the general export price (f.a.s.) for exports, and the general import price (f.o.b.) for imports, shown as point C in Figure 1 and calculated as $100 in Table 1.

The definition of transactions value (TV) is very similar to that in IRC Section 482 for the comparable uncontrolled price (CUP) method; thus, TV and CUP are roughly equivalent. One key difference lies in the types of comparables that are allowed for purposes of constructing the arm's length price. For TV, the appropriate comparison is with identical or similar products exported to the United States under similar circumstances as the imported product. For CUP, the appropriate comparison is with similar transactions between unrelated parties under similar circumstances to the intrafirm transaction. Two differences stand out: (1) for TV, the comparables are other imported goods whereas for CUP, the comparables are other transactions (whether domestic or international)[19]; (2) for TV, the comparables do not have to be between unrelated parties whereas for CUP, only unrelated party transactions are included. Thus, TV is both narrower (only imports versus all transactions) and broader (all parties versus only unrelated parties) than CUP.

Deductive Value (DV) Method

In the United States, the *deductive value method* calculates the transfer price by subtracting a gross profit margin from a retail price (US Customs 1999, Ch.X). Thus, DV is roughly equivalent to the resale price method under IRC section 482. The appropriate retail price is one of the following prices:

(i) the unit price of the same or a similar product, sold in the same condition as the imported product, in the greatest aggregate quantity at or about the date of importation, but no later than 90 days after importation; or

(ii) for products not sold in the same condition as imported and not sold before the 90th day after importation of the merchandise to be appraised, the price is the unit price at which the merchandise being appraised, after further processing, is sold in the greatest aggregate quantity before the 180th day after the date of importation.

The "greatest aggregate quantity" unit price means the unit price when the product is sold to unrelated persons at the first commercial level after importation in the case of (i), or after further processing in the case of (ii), in a total volume that is greater than the volume sold at any other price and sufficient in volume to establish the unit price. Packing costs incurred by the importer can be added to the unit price, if such costs are not otherwise included.

The deductive value method then subtracts the following items from the unit price:

(a) a gross profit margin to cover profit and general expenses[20], or any commission usually paid or agreed to be paid, in connection with US sales of imported products that are of the same class or kind as the merchandise to be appraised, regardless of the country of exportation;

(b) the actual and associated costs of international transportation and insurance connected with shipping the product from the country of exportation to the United States;

(c) the actual and associated costs of transportation and insurance incurred within the United States between the point of importation and the place of delivery, if such costs are not included as a general expense in (a);

(d) US customs duties and other federal taxes currently payable on the imported merchandise, and any federal excise taxes for which US vendors are normally liable;

(e) where valuation is based on further processing in (ii) above, the value added by the processing the product after importation. Deductions for value added in processing must be based on objective and quantifiable data relating to the cost of the work performed, using accepted US industry standards as the basis for the deduction.

In (a), the gross profit margin must be consistent with the usual profit and general expenses reflected in US sales of imported merchandise of the same class or kind. In determining the gross margin, US sales of the narrowest group or range of imported merchandise of the same class or kind, including the merchandise being appraised, for which sufficient information can be provided, must be examined. State and local taxes imposed on importation are treated as general expenses. Any sale to a person who supplies an assist in connection with the production or sale for export of the appraised merchandise must be disregarded for purposes of determining the deductive value.

Computed Value (CV) Method

In the United States, the *computed value method* is constructed by adding together (US Customs 1999, Ch. IV):

(i) the cost or value of materials plus fabrication or other processing costs;

(ii) a markup for profit and general expenses (gross profit markup) equal that usually reflected in sales of merchandise of the same class or kind as the imported merchandise that are made by producers in the country of exportation for export to the United States;

(iii) any assists[21] not included in (i) or (ii); and

(iv) packing costs.

This method again looks very similar to one of the transfer pricing methods in IRC section 482 – cost plus. In calculating the CV method, any internal tax imposed by the exporting country should be excluded if the tax is refunded upon exportation. The GATT Customs Valuation Code allows governments to choose whether or not to include transport costs from the place of export to the place of importation, associated loading, unloading and handling charges, and insurance costs. The US approach ignores these costs and focuses on the free on board (f.o.b.) price at the point of exportation.

Other Methods

In the case where none of the above trio (TV, DV or CV) methods can be applied, the US customs regulations allow (as do the IRS regulations) for the use of "other methods" if they can be justified. Note, however, that US customs does not explicitly include any profit-based comparisons such as the comparable profits method or profits splits, which have become so popular in the United States since they were introduced in the 1994 revised section 482 transfer pricing regulations.

Implications for the BLS International Price Program

Customs or Tax: Whose Prices Should be Used in the IPP?

Going back to the theoretical incentives for manipulating transfer prices when the MNE is faced with tax differentials and customs duties, as outlined above in equation (16), the implication is that US Customs should be concerned about underinvoicing (in order to avoid the tariff), while the IRS should be concerned about overinvoicing (in order to avoid the high US tax). If the MNE is constrained to use one transfer price that is known to both government bodies, then both units should expect the same pricing behavior and adjust their own regulatory positions based on that information. This suggests that the regulated transfer price **W** set by both organizations should be the same and thus, that either pricing program should provide an acceptable basis for the IPP. However, several factors suggest that equivalence between the customs and tax transfer pricing programs is unlikely to occur in practice:

- *Differences in timing:* Valuation of international intrafirm imports by US Customs, as we have seen above, normally takes place no later than 90 days after importation. The IRS, on the other hand, might not examine the MNE's income tax statements for up to three years after filing of the tax forms. Contemporaneous documentation requirements, introduced in 1994, now require MNEs to document their transfer pricing policies in accordance with IRC section 482 methods at the end of each tax year. This suggests that timing differences may be shorter now than in the past.

- *Differences in definitions*: In 1986, the US Congress passed IRC section 1059A requiring the transfer price for inbound transfers for income tax purposes to be no higher than the price for customs duty purposes. Thus the US Customs price sets an effective upper bound for merchandise import prices for tax purposes. Section 1059A has been problematic in practice because the customs valuation is based on the general import price (f.o.b.) in the country of export, whereas the income tax valuation is based on the total cost to the importing firm. In Table 2, the customs price would be $100, whereas the tax price would be $135.

- *Different comparables*: The customs valuation methods are very similar to the early trio of transfer pricing methods in the corporate income tax act: CUP (transactions value), resale price (deductive value) and cost plus (computed value). However, the comparables used to determine an arm's length price differ. Only imported products are considered for tariff purposes, while all transactions (domestic and international) are included for tax purposes. On the other hand, only transactions between unrelated firms can be considered for tax purposes, while all transactions regardless of ownership are included for customs purposes.

- *Different methods*: Section 482 now includes profit-based methods such as profit splits and the comparable profits method. It is almost impossible for profit-based comparables to develop a meaningful transfer price for a transaction in a particular product; that is, profit-based transfer prices do not provide a "micro level" (product/transaction) level transfer price. These methods are more useful for "broad-brush comparisons" at the level of the strategic business unit. Since CPM and profit splits are becoming increasingly popular methods in the United States (Ernst & Young 1999), transfer prices under the corporate income tax should become less useful for the BLS international price program, relative to the US Customs valuation methods.

- *Sharing of information:* There is growing cooperation between the IRS and US Customs. The two agencies are now sharing information through joint access to data bases. In practice, the exchange is one way because the IRS is prohibited by law from sharing private corporate income tax returns with any other agency including US Customs, so that the flow of information is from US Customs to the IRS. As a result, international tax auditors now (or will soon) have access to the customs valuation for US merchandise imports.

Due to these differences, we argue that the US Customs valuation methods provide a better approximation of the *actual price paid or payable* than the IRS valuation methods for income taxation. This has clear implications for the BLS international price program.

If the focus of the BLS international price program is to determine how international prices of US exports and imports move (past, present and future), and the impact of these price changes on US competitiveness, the key issue is the best measure of the actual price paid or payable by US importers and the actual price received or receivable by US exporters. Where intrafirm trade is concerned, the actual price is the transfer price, regardless of the method (price based, cost based) incurred or received by the US firm. For US merchandise imports, the US Customs valuation is the best measure available, and also the measure that most closely corresponds in theory and practice to the desired price index.

If Customs Prices Are Necessary, Are They Also Sufficient?

However, for US merchandise and service exports, and for US trade in intangible assets, the US customs valuation is much less help than for merchandise import trade. If neither the US Customs nor the IRS transfer price is a close proxy for the price received or receivable by US exporters for their international intrafirm transactions, what other alternatives are available? One insight is provided by US exports to Canada. Since 1991, US Customs has substituted Canadian import prices for US export prices on the grounds that the Canadian import prices are a superior measure, that is, more attention is paid by regulatory customs authorities on trade inflows than outflows. As Table 2 and Figure 2 show, the general export price (f.a.s.), general import price (f.o.b.) and transaction value should all three be the same price – in theory. However, in practice, the US Bureau of the Census has found US export prices to be better proxied by Canadian import prices. This suggests that one possibility is for the BLS to explore similar arrangements with other OECD member countries, using their import prices as substitutes for US export prices and in construction of the US export price index.

A second alternative is now coming about because of the changing role of US Customs in enforcing the rules of origin in the North American Free Trade Agreement (NAFTA). Because rules of origin apply to both imports and exports, customs agents may be developing better expertise at valuing both inflows and outflows of international trade. New databases may emerge that better track the transfer prices for both US exports and imports, although the focus again will be primarily on merchandise trade flows.

Other BLS Issues re Transfer Pricing Policies

- *Are the current five transfer pricing categories on the BLS survey sufficient?*

No, the BLS list of transfer pricing methods should be changed to correspond more closely with the US Customs and IRS methods. An appropriate listing might be: market price (CUP, transactions value), resale price (resale price, deductive value), cost based (cost plus, computed value), profit based (profit split, comparable profits method) and none of the above.

- *If a company changes its transfer pricing methodology, should BLS "link" out the change?*

No, changes in a firm's transfer pricing policy (e.g., from market based to cost based) have a variety of motivations (e.g., economics, strategy, taxes) and are reasonably common. The item should not be omitted simply because the MNE changed its transfer pricing policy.

- *Should the BLS use statistical tests on "outliers"?*

The IRS uses statistical tests as "smell tests" for transfer price manipulation; large outliers are investigated for possible tax avoidance/evasion. Large outliers could also be evidence of inaccurate reporting of prices. More generally, the size and direction of the over and underreporting of intrafirm transactions is of interest. For example, is the amount and direction of transfer price manipulation growing or falling over time? Do outliers occur more frequently with certain products and/or in trade with particular countries? Therefore, econometric testing of the international price indexes may be useful on several accounts.

- *Should the BLS be concerned about currency issues; transfer prices sometimes overcompensate for ER changes, in others undercompensate?*

The degree of compensation depends on whether MNEs pass exchange rate changes through in terms of market prices. This is an important subject for researchers; that is, do firms simply pass through exchange rate changes or do they price to market? Does intrafirm trade pass through more or less exchange rate changes compared to arm's length trade? This information, as evidenced in the IPP, is important for researchers as it provides information on the marketing strategies and competitiveness of US and foreign firms. Therefore, exchange rate pass through should not be obscured or removed from the data.

- *How should the BLS handle mixed decreases and increases in transfer prices for otherwise homogeneous goods?*

As we have seen above, transfer prices are likely differ between firms and across products. The most general differences are between market and cost based pricing policies. There are many reasons why purchasing power parity (the law of one price) should not hold for intrafirm trade since Hirshleifer's Rule only applies to MNEs in restrictive circumstances. Therefore, transfer prices rising and falling for the same commodity, even between different affiliates of the same MNE group, should generally have an economic or business strategy explanation and not be cause for concern.

- *How should the BLS handle large transfer price changes that seem random to "balance the books"?*

First, many large transfer pricing changes have simple explanations. If the large change is accompanied by a reported change in the pricing method (e.g., from market to cost based), this explains the change. End-of-year changes (a different type of seasonality!!) probably are corporate income tax driven. If the intrafirm trade is with a country that prohibits foreign currency repatriation, transfer pricing can be used to move funds out of the country. Exchange rate changes may also be the reason. Second, even if large random changes in transfer prices do occur, the BLS should keep these transfer prices in the IPP and not remove them unless they significantly affect the index (e.g. the size of intrafirm trade is a very high percent of total weight for the index).

CONCLUSIONS

This paper has explored the question: what impacts can international intrafirm trade have on the calculation of the US export and import price indexes? We reviewed the current BLS international price index program, and provided a simple example of international transportation chain, showing the possible price indexes that could be constructed as a product moves from the factory gate in the exporting country to consumers in the importing country. We developed a theoretical model of the MNE's optimal intrafirm trade and transfer pricing choices under free trade, tariffs and profit taxes. We also analyzed the transfer pricing regulations employed by customs and tax authorities to prevent transfer price manipulation, with particular reference to US customs and tax regulations.

Our paper shows that the BLS international price program does have a strong economic foundation, not only for international trade between unrelated parties but also for trade between related firms. For both theoretical and practical reasons, we recommend continuing to use the US Customs valuation methodology for valuing US merchandise imports. We do make some suggestions for change. For example, the list of transfer pricing methods could correspond more closely with the US Customs and IRS list of methods. Other alternatives such as substituting foreign country import prices for US merchandise export prices, particularly with other OECD countries, could usefully be explored.

The "bottom line" for the BLS international price program is to find the best measures for the actual prices paid or payable for imports and received or receivable for exports. This mandate applies to every national agency that is assigned the responsibility of producing international price indexes. Transfer pricing and intrafirm trade add significant -- but manageable -- complications to this task.

.

<hr width="40%" align="left">

ENDNOTES

[1] Details provided by correspondence with William Alterman and discussions with BLS staff. See also Clausing (2000) although her data set does not distinguish between pre and post February 1998 prices.

[2] The IPP also imputs prices where they are not supplied (see Feenstra & Diewert, 2000) and adjusts for seasonality (see Alterman, Diewert & Feenstra, 1999).

[3] Export/import subsidies are easily modeled by changing the sign on the trade taxes.

[4] Except in the case of exports to Canada, where Canadian Customs import data is used instead of US export data.

[5] The analogy is based on the international tax literature, which distinguishes between capital export neutrality (all residents in the capital exporting country should earn the same after-tax return on investments abroad as they do at home) and capital import neutrality (all investments in the capital importing country should earn the same after-tax return regardless of the ownership of the investment). See Eden (1998: 73-79).

[6] The reader interested in services and intangibles is directed to Chapter 5 in Eden (1998).

[7] Note that both firms are assumed to be price makers in their respective domestic markets. We relax this assumption below for the exporting firm.

[8] In effect, the transactions costs modeled here are the net difference between international and domestic transactions costs.

[9] Note that the final price to the consumer depends on the *average revenue* curve, which lies above the *marginal revenue* and *net marginal revenue* curves.

[10] The rule also holds in the case where the external price lies below the initial transfer price.

[11] See Eden (1998: Ch. 5) for more details.

[12] We ignore the complications of home country taxation of foreign source income.

[13] Note, however, one should not automatically assume that the MNE's transfer prices are designed especially to avoid government barriers. As Colbert & Spicer (1995) show, asset specificity considerations, which are efficiency based in nature, may be the overriding consideration driving the MNE's transfer pricing policy decisions. Cultural differences may also affect the MNE's pricing policies. For example, Buckley & Hughes (1998) argue that target costing techniques and the ethnocentricity of Japanese MNEs cause a preference for income shifting to Japan even though corporate tax rates are higher in Japan than most OECD countries.

[14] Note that, in theory, p^e and W should be the same price since both are measures of the arm's length price. However, in practice, this is unlikely to be the case unless the CUP method is used (see below).

[15] Because I have written on this topic so extensively elsewhere (Eden 1998: Chs. 8 and 9), the discussion in this section is less technical and detailed compared with the discussion of the US customs regulations.

[16] The OECD 1995 guidelines recommend the Transactional Net Margin Method as preferable to the Comparable Profit Method. The IRS regards the two methods as the same. For more information, see OECD (1995) and Eden (forthcoming, 1998).

[17] Appraised value and dutiable value have different meanings. Appraised value is the final determination, by US Customs under TAA section 402, as the full value of the imported merchandise. Dutiable value refers to that portion, if any, of the appraised value of the imported article upon which duty is actually assessed.

[18] "Related parties" covers a variety of relationships, including members of the same family, any officer or director of an organization, partners, employer and employee, any person directly or

indirectly owning or controlling 5 percent or more of the outstanding voting stock or shares of an organization, persons associated in business where one is the sole agent, distributor or concessionaire of the other.

[19] The rule, for tax purposes, is that comparables should come from the destination market. Thus, comparables for outbound transactions should come from the foreign country while inbound transactions use domestic comparables. Where these are not readily available and market differentials can be measured, the other market can be used to establish an arm's length range of prices. The transfer pricing method also matters. For example, the resale price method requires comparables from the importing country market; whereas the cost plus method requires comparables from the exporting country market (see Eden, 1998; IRS, 1994).

[20] "General expenses" are costs of doing business that either cannot be allocated to the particular product or are not related to its production/manufacture, such as administrative salaries, insurance, advertising, salesperson commissions or expenses.

[21] "Assist" means something (e.g., materials, tools, engineering services) "supplied directly or indirectly, and free of charge or at reduced cost, by the buyer of imported merchandise for use in connection with the production or the sale for export to the United States of the merchandise" (US Customs, 1999: Ch. I: 1).

REFERENCES

Alterman, William. 1997a. "A Comparison of the Export and Producer Price Indexes for Semiconductors". Presented at the National Bureau of Economic Research Summer Institute, July.

Alterman, William. 1997b. "Are producer prices good proxies for export prices?" *Monthly Labor Review* October: 18-32.

Alterman, William, W. Erwin Diewert and Robert C. Feenstra. 1999. *International Trade Price Indexes and Seasonal Commodities*. Washington, DC: Bureau of Labor Statistics, US Department of Labor.

Bonturi, Marcos and Kiichiro Fukasaku. 1993. "Globalization and Intrafirm Trade: An Empirical Note". *OECD Economic Studies*. No. 20 (spring): 145-59.

Buckley, Peter J. and Jane Frecknall Hughes. 1998. "Transfer pricing and economic functions analysis: the Japanese paradigm". *Applied Economics* 30.5: 621-30.

Cameron, Richard A. 1998. *Intrafirm Trade of Canadian-Based Foreign Transnational Companies*. Industry Canada Working Paper No. 26. Ottawa: Industry Canada.

Clausing, Kimberly. 2000. The Behavior of Intrafirm Trade in US International Price Data. Presented at the Bureau of Labor Statistics Conference on *Issues in Measuring Price Change and Consumption* in Washington, DC, June 5-8, 2000.

Colbert, Gary J. and Barry H. Spicer. 1995. "A Multi-case Investigation of a Theory of the Transfer Pricing Process". *Accounting, Organizations and Society* 20.6: 423-56.

Covari, Ronald and Robert Wisner. 1993. *Foreign Multinationals and Canada's International Competitiveness*. Industry Canada Working Paper No. 16. Ottawa: Industry Canada.

Diewert, Erwin. 1985. "Transfer Pricing and Economic Efficiency". In Alan Rugman and

Lorraine Eden, editors. *Multinationals and Transfer Pricing*. London and New York: Croom Helm and St. Martins Press.

Eden, Lorraine. Forthcoming. "Taxes, Transfer Pricing and the Multinational Enterprise". In *The Oxford Handbook of International Business*, Alan Rugman and Thomas Brewer (editors). Oxford, UK: Oxford University Press.

Eden, Lorraine. 1998. *Taxing Multinationals: Transfer Pricing and Corporate Income Taxation in North America*. Toronto: University of Toronto Press.

Eden, Lorraine. 1985. "The Microeconomics of Transfer Pricing". In Alan Rugman and Lorraine Eden, editors. *Multinationals and Transfer Pricing*. London and New York: Croom Helm and St. Martins Press.

Encarnation, Dennis. 1993. "Intra-firm Trade in North America and the European Economy". In Lorraine Eden, editor, *Multinationals in North America*. Calgary: University of Calgary Press.

Ernst & Young. 1999. *Transfer Pricing: 1999 Global Survey*. Ernst & Young International.

Feenstra, Robert C. and W. Erwin Diewert. 2000. Imputation and Price Indexes: Theory and Evidence from the International Price Program. Presented at the Bureau of Labor Statistics Conference on *Issues in Measuring Price Change and Consumption* in Washington, DC, June 5-8, 2000.

Hines, James. 1999. "Lessons from Behavioral Responses to International Taxation". *National Tax Journal* 52.2: 305-xx.

Hipple, F. Steb. 1990a. "Multinational Companies and International Trade: The Impact of Intrafirm Shipments on US Foreign Trade, 1977-82". *Journal of International Business Studies*, 3rd Quarter: 495-503.

Hipple, F. Steb. 1990b. "The Measurement of International Trade Related to Multinational Companies". *American Economic Review* (December): 1263-70.

Hirshleifer, Jack. 1957. "Economics of the Divisionalized Firm." *Journal of Business* 30: 96-108.

Hirshleifer, Jack. 1956. "On the Economics of Transfer Pricing." *Journal of Business* 29: 172-83.

Horst, Thomas. 1971. "Theory of the Multinational Firm: Optimal Behaviour Under Differing Tariff and Tax Rates". *Journal of Political Economy* 79 (September/October): 1059-72.

Krajewski, Stephen. 1992. *Intrafirm Trade and the New North American Business Dynamic.* Conference Board of Canada Report 88-92. Ottawa: Conference Board of Canada.

Mataloni, Raymond. 1999. "US Multinational Companies: Operations in 1997". *Survey of Current Business.*

OECD. 1995. *Transfer Pricing Guidelines for Multinational Enterprises and Tax Administrations.* Paris: OECD. Looseleaf updates.

Rangan, Subramanian. 2000. Tranquility in the Midst of Turbulence: US Multinationals' Intrafirm Trade, 1966-97. Presented at the Bureau of Labor Statistics Conference on *Issues in Measuring Price Change and Consumption* in Washington, DC, June 5-8, 2000.

United Nations Conference on Trade and Development (UNCTAD). 1999. *Transfer Pricing.* New York: UNCTAD.

US Bureau of Labor Statistics (BLS). 1999a. Chapter 2, "The Conceptual Framework of the International Price Indexes". Draft manuscript.

US Bureau of Labor Statistics (BLS). 1999b. Chapter 6, "The Outputs and Uses of IPP Data". Draft manuscript.

US Bureau of Labor Statistics (BLS). 1997. *BLS Handbook of Methods.* Washington, DC: US

Department of Labor.

US Census. 1999. *Related Party Trade - 1998.* Washington, DC: US Census Bureau.

US Customs Administration. 1999. *Customs Valuation Encyclopedia, 1980 - 1998.* Washington, DC: Department of the Treasury.

US Internal Revenue Service. 1994. *Intercompany Transfer Pricing Regulations under Section 482. T.D. 8552.* Washington, DC: US Government Printing Office.

Whichard, Obie and Jeffrey Lowe. 1998. "The statistics corner: an ownership-based supplement to the US balance of payments account". *Business Economics* 33.2: 59-67.

Whichard, Obie and Jeffrey Lowe. 1995. "An ownership-based disaggregation of the US current account, 1982-93". *Survey of Current Business* 75.10: 52-62.

Zeile, William J. 1997. "US Intrafirm Trade in Goods". *Survey of Current Business*, February: 23-38.

Table 1: Comparison of the US International and Producer Price Programs

	Export Price Index	Import Price Index	Producer Price Index
Target universe	Value of US exports for all goods and services sold by US residents to foreign residents.	Value of US imports for all goods and services bought by US residents from foreign residents.	Value of shipments by US industry for all goods and services produced in the US.
Purpose of BLS program	To sample and estimate export price changes across products in order to construct real export component of US NIPA.	To sample and estimate import price changes across products in order to construct real import component of US NIPA.	To sample and estimate price changes across industries in order to construct net output indexes.
Data source for the sampling frames	*Goods:* BCENS trade tapes of Shippers' Export Declarations filed with US Customs Service.* *Services:* Individual sources.	*Goods:* Customs trade tapes of Import Forms filed with US Customs Service. *Services:* Individual sources.	Unemployment Insurance file of US producers.
Geographic Scope	US, US territories, bonded warehouses and foreign trade zones.	US only.	US only.
Classification system	Samples drawn according to GATT Harmonized System (HS) commodity grouping.	Samples drawn according to GATT Harmonized System (HS) commodity classification.	Samples drawn by industry SIC classification.
Sample Respondents	Voluntary sample of US producers, brokers, freight forwarders and any other establishment completing export documentation.	Voluntary sample of US buyers, brokers, freight forwarders and any other establishment completing import documentation.	Voluntary sample of US producers by SIC classification.
Stage of processing	All exported products regardless of the stage of processing.	All imported products regardless of the stage of processing.	Nets out shipments of intermediate goods.
Price basis	f.a.s. price at US port, including inland freight, insurance, etc. to bring product to point of exit.	f.o.b. price at foreign port, excluding duties, insurance, etc., to bring product into the US.	US factory gate price.
Number of items	11,000 **	12,000 **	100,000
Treatment of intrafirm trade	Before February 1998, BLS used only transfer prices that trended with the market; after that date began to use all transfer prices.		Intrafirm trade between affiliates in the same industry not included.

* Except for Canada, where Canadian Customs import data have been used instead of US export data since 1991.

** International price data (exports plus imports) are collected monthly for 20,000-25,000 goods and every three months for 1,500-2,000 service items (BLS 1997.157).

Source: author's modification of Alterman (1997b: 20) based on Alterman, Diewert & Feenstra (1999), BLS (1997, 1999a, 1999b).

55

Table 2: An Example of the Transportation Chain

	Location *	Amount
Foreign manufacturer's standard cost		$ 55.00
+ Gross profit mark-up over standard cost (20%)		11.00
Foreign manufacturer's factory gate price	A	66.00
+ Inland freight, insurance & fees		14.00
= Pre-Tax Export Price	B	$80.00
+ Export tax (25% of the pre-tax export price)		20.00
= *General Export Price (f.a.s.) (water's edge for exit)*	C	*$100.00*
= *General Import Price (f.o.b.) a.k.a. Transactions Value*	C	*$100.00*
+ Cross-border (international) freight, insurance & fees		15.00
= *Pre-Tariff Import Price (c.i.f.) (water's edge for entry)*	D	*$115.00*
+ Customs duties (10% of the Transaction Price)		10.00
= Post-Tariff Import Price	E	*$125.00*
+ Inland freight, insurance & fees		10.00
= Domestic distributor's standard cost	F	*$135.00*
+ Distributor's profit margin (10% of final market price)		15.00
= Final market price to consumer	G	$150.00

* The letters in the Location column refer to points in Figures 1 and 2.

56

Table 3: Which Price Will the MNE Choose?

	No External Market	External Market	
		No Interdependencies in Supply or Demand	Interdependencies in Supply and/or Demand
No Tariffs or Taxes	λ the shadow price, the external marginal cost of the exporting affiliate	p^e the arm's length price, the external price available on the open market	p^e the arm's length price adjusted for the impact of interdependencies within the MNE group
Tariffs and/or Taxes — No regulated price **W**	p^* the profit maximizing price, taking into account taxes and tariffs.	p^* the profit maximizing price, taking into account the external market price, taxes and tariffs.	p^* the profit maximizing price, taking into account the external market price, taxes and tariffs, and interdependencies within the MNE group.
Tariffs and/or Taxes — Regulated price **W**	**W** the regulated price	**W** the regulated price	**W** the regulated price

Figure 1: The International Transportation Chain

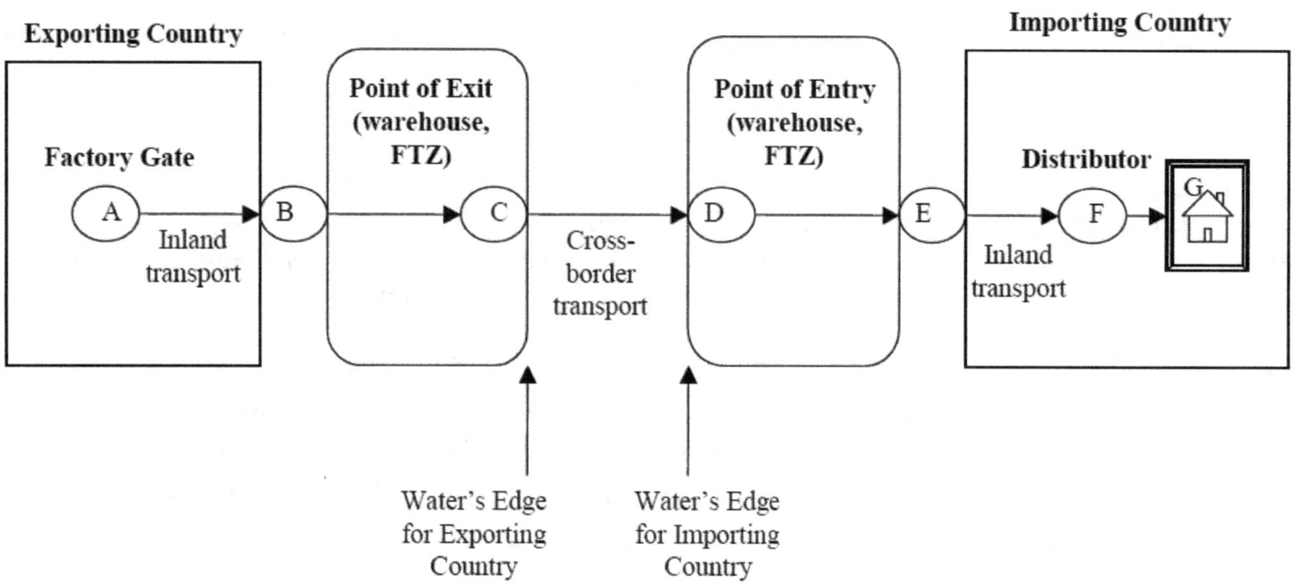

Exporting Country

Factory Gate

(A)

Inland transport

(B)

Point of Exit
(warehouse,
FTZ)

(C)

Water's Edge
for Exporting
Country

Cross-border transport

Water's Edge
for Importing
Country

(D)

Point of Entry
(warehouse,
FTZ)

(E)

Inland transport

Distributor

(F)

(G)

Importing Country

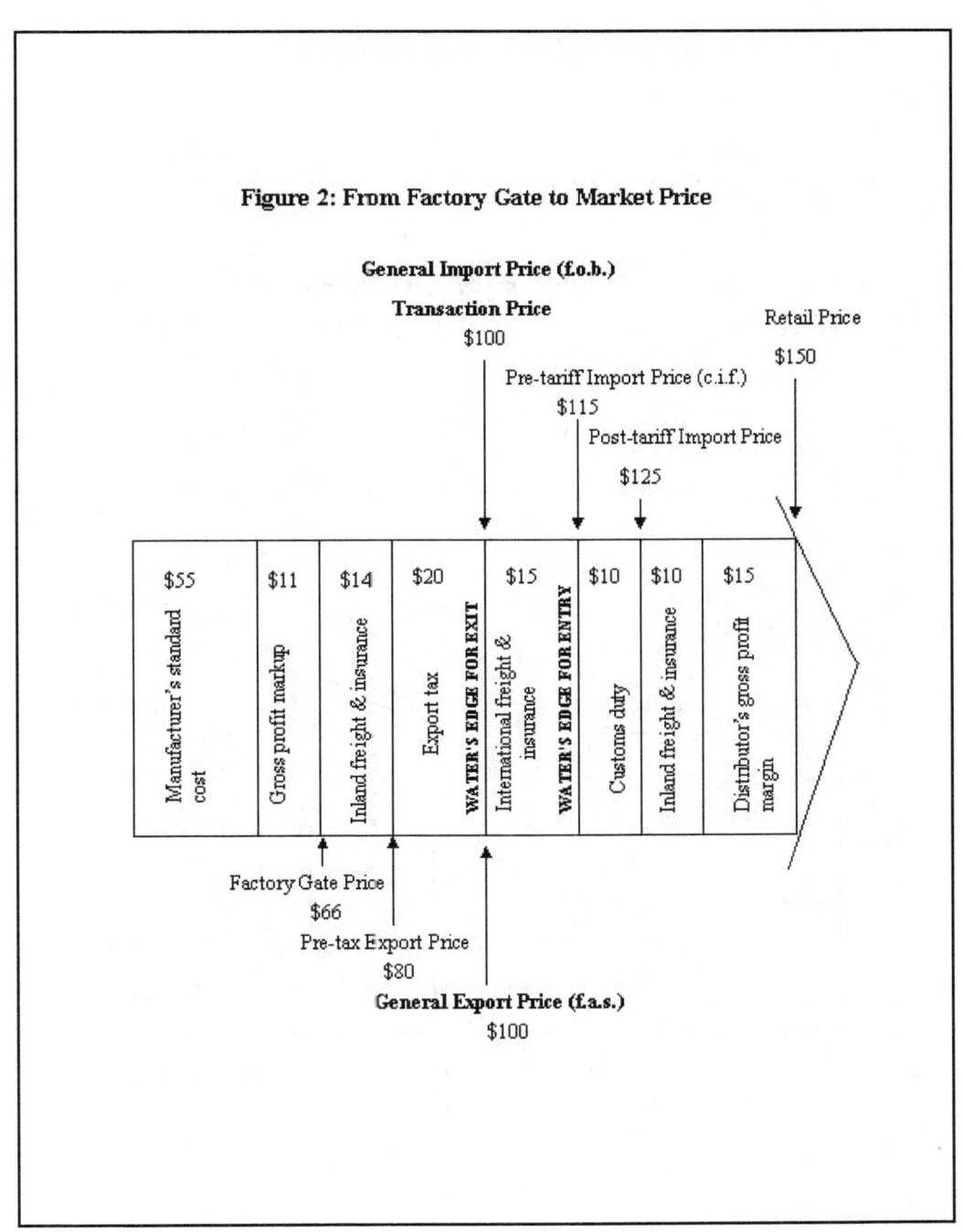

Figure 2: From Factory Gate to Market Price

Figure 3: Pricing in Arm's Length versus Related Party Markets

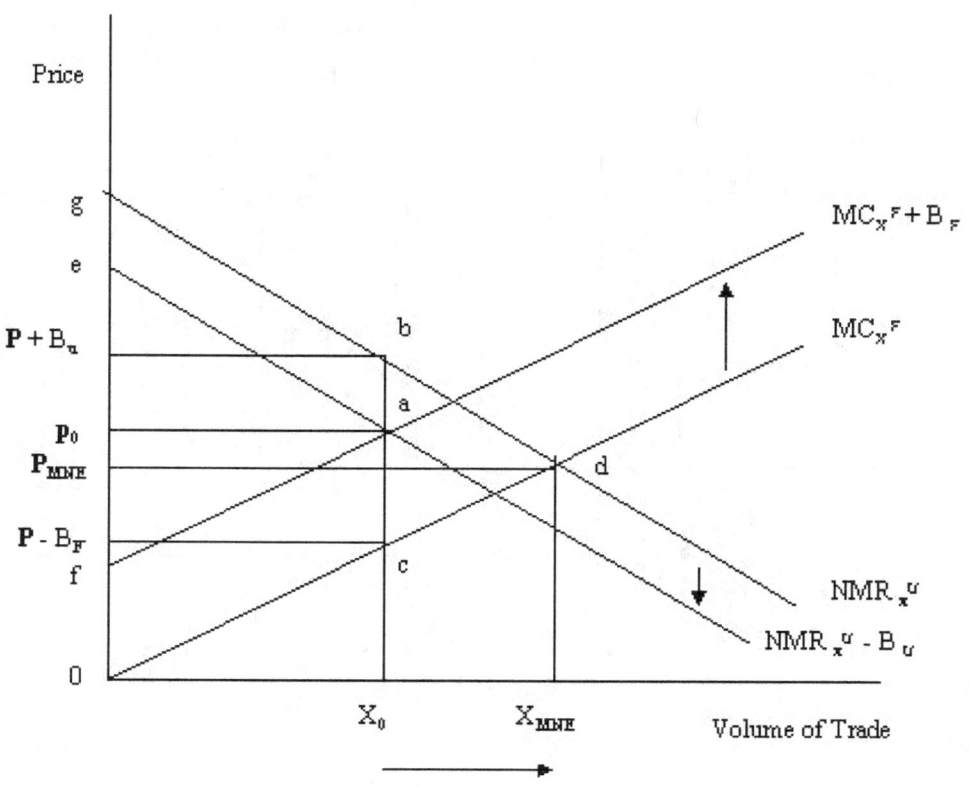